What Is Your
Dog
Really Thinking?

WHAT IS YOUR DOG REALLY THINKING?

Illustrations by Dannyboy

Text by Sophie Johnson

An Hachette UK Company
www.hachette.co.uk

Summersdale Publishers Ltd
Part of Octopus Publishing Group Limited
Carmelite House
50 Victoria Embankment
LONDON
EC4Y 0DZ
UK

www.summersdale.com

Printed and bound in China

ISBN: 978-1-84953-916-6

Substantial discounts on bulk quantities of Summersdale books are available to corporations, professional associations and other organisations. For details contact general enquiries: telephone: +44 (0) 1243 771107 or email: enquiries@summersdale.com.

What Is Your
Dog
Really Thinking?

COOL FUTURE SCARF, DAD,
BUT I CAN'T GET TO MY ITCH.

Dannyboy
and Sophie Johnson

YOU SHAVED A PUG?
YOU SHAVED IT SMOOTH?

YOU SAID YOU WERE LOOKING FOR THE BACON.
I FOUND YOU SOME. I DON'T GET YOU HUMANS.

MUST... MAKE... PERFECT... BED...
OOH! NOPE, NEARLY HAD IT...

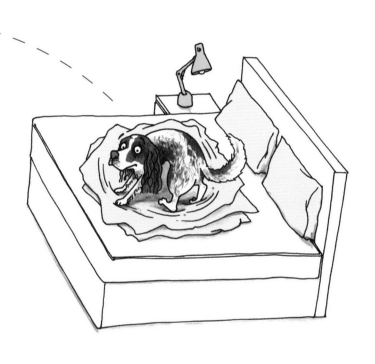

THREE MORE SECONDS
AND I'M CALLING
THE RSPCA.

EXCUSE ME, SiR! YOUR BRAKE LIGHT'S OUT!
IT'S A POTENTIAL DEATH TRAP!

THIS IS YOUR THREE-SECOND WARNING!
COME QUICKLY IF YOU WANT YOUR
CARPET TO BE SAVED!

CHARMED. BUT HAVEN'T
WE MET BEFORE?

CK ONE? WHAT IS THIS, THE NINETIES?

I UNDERSTAND YOU DIDN'T WANT TO SHARE
YOUR DINNER WITH ME A MINUTE AGO. HAVE
YOU CHANGED YOUR MIND NOW I'VE PUT MY
HEAD ON YOUR LEG? HOW ABOUT NOW?

I'D LIKE TO THANK BEYONCÉ,
MY SPIRIT HUMAN, FOR SHOWING
ME HOW TO BE A DIVA.

OH MAN, I SURE AM EXCITED TO GO IN THE C.A.R. AND FIND OUT WHO THIS V.E.T. GUY IS.

I DON'T KNOW WHAT THIS HORRID
FRUITY, FLOWERY SMELL IS, BUT
NEVER FEAR! I SHALL RETURN THE
FLOOR FLUFF TO YOUR FAVOURITE
EAU DE DOG IN NO TIME.

I'VE STILL GOT MY BALLS.

THE WOMAN IS GONE AT LAST.
IT'S JUST YOU AND ME, PAL.

PLAY iT COOL, KEN.
PLAY iT COOL.

THERE YOU ARE! BEFORE
YOU GO IN THE KITCHEN,
REMEMBER THAT I LOVE YOU.

HUMAN! I JUST DREAMT WE WERE AT THE VET.
AND THE CAT WAS THERE BUT IT WASN'T THE CAT,
IT WAS NOEL EDMONDS. WHAT DOES IT MEAN!?

OH, GIANT FURLESS PACK LEADER,
iF ONLY YOU COULD WOOF. I WONDER
WHAT'S GOING ON IN THAT TINY BRAIN
OF YOURS...

YES! POO JOURNEY!

YOU JUST SLEEP, LITTLE
SAUSAGE. RAMBO'S HERE
TO PROTECT YOU.

YOU'VE BEEN PLAY FIGHTING
WITH SANDRA HAVEN'T YOU?!

HI! JUST TO SAY QUICKLY I MISS YOU AND I LOVE YOU! BYE!

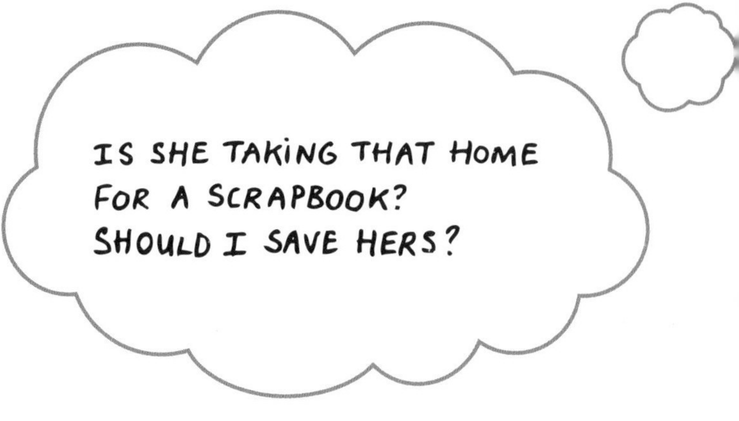
IS SHE TAKING THAT HOME
FOR A SCRAPBOOK?
SHOULD I SAVE HERS?

IF HE DIDN'T WANT TO SLEEP IN IT, WHY DID HE BUY IT? SILLY HUMAN.

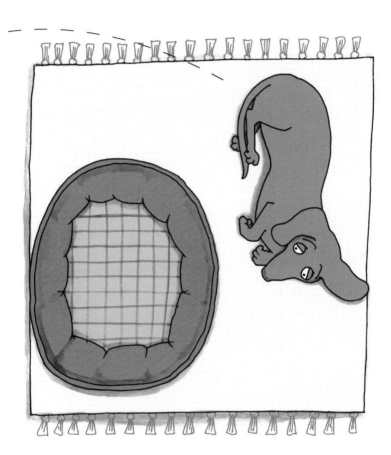

NOOOOOO! I'VE ONLY JUST GOT MYSELF
SMELLING NICELY OF FOX POO AND YOU'RE
GOING TO RUIN IT ALL!

UPWARDS RAIN iS MY BESTEST!

IT'S A TAD SALTY THIS WEEK,
BUT IT'LL DO.

I BEAT BUSTER! THIS'LL EARN
ME SOME SERIOUS STREET CRED.

I AM BOUNTIFUL, I AM BEAUTIFUL,
I AM BLISSFUL, I AM BARRY.

SOME RED GERANIUMS HERE WOULD BE RAVISHING. NO! YELLOW TULIPS!

BUT LAST YEAR I WAS 14?!
AM I A TIME WIZARD?!

SO YOU'RE THE QUIET TYPE, HUH?
FANCY A BISCUIT SOMETIME?

What Is Your
Cat
Really Thinking?

WE NEED TO TALK ABOUT
YOUR CULINARY EFFORTS.

FELIX

Dannyboy
and Sophie Johnson

If you're interested in finding out more about our books,
find us on Facebook at **Summersdale Publishers**
and follow us on Twitter at **@Summersdale.**

www.summersdale.com

WHAT IS YOUR CAT REALLY THINKING?

Dannyboy
and Sophie Johnson

ISBN: 978 1 84953 948 7

Hardback

£6.99

The secrets of the moggy world are out!

Find out what your curious kitty really thinks when you try
to play with them, why they love knocking things off tables,
and why they get really cheesed off when your culinary skills
fall short of their expectations.